BEYOND THE ORPHAN TRAIN
A True Adventure

Donna Nordmark Aviles

Wasteland Press
Louisville, KY USA
www.wastelandpress.com

BEYOND THE ORPHAN TRAIN
A True Adventure
By Donna Nordmark Aviles

Second Printing – September 2007
ISBN: 1-932852-94-8

Printed in the U.S.A.

Dedicated in honor and memory of America's Orphan Train Children – especially Oliver and Edward. May their stories never be forgotten and may we learn from them the value of EVERY child.

Joseph Petr Sod House – Circa 1913

INTRODUCTION

In 1853 The Children's Aid Society was established to address the needs of thousands of homeless and neglected children in New York City. Between 1854 and 1929, more than 100,000 children were sent via train from the city to farming communities in the Midwest. Recognizing the need for labor in the expanding farm country, it was believed that the farmers would welcome the orphans and take them into their families. This was the forerunner of today's foster care system.

In 1906 Oliver Nordmark and his younger brother Edward were placed on an Orphan Train after living in The Children's Village of the New York Juvenile Asylum. Oliver was eight and Edward was just five years old. Their earliest adventures are the subject of my first book, *FLY LITTLE BIRD, FLY! The True Story of Oliver Nordmark & America's Orphan Trains.*

This book is the companion story to *FLY LITTLE BIRD, FLY!* Picking up where that story left off, *BEYOND THE ORPHAN TRAIN* will answer all the reader's questions such as: Where does Oliver go? What happens to Edward? Do the brothers find each other? While it is not necessary to read *FLY LITTLE BIRD, FLY!* to fully appreciate this second book, you may enjoy reading about the boy's earliest years too. If after reading the stories you have unanswered questions, **www.orphantrainbook.bravehost.com** is a website where you can enter your question in the Guestbook and receive an answer online.

These true adventures are based on tape recordings made by Oliver Nordmark and told to his youngest son Benjamin, my father. I hope you enjoy the tale....

CONTENTS

CHAPTER ONE:
THE TRAIN TRAVELER

"Hey you, Sonny! Down off that engine!" the railroad cop called out to Oliver. "Get over here!"

The freight train that Oliver had been clinging to through the last three little towns had come to a stop on a siding – a piece of track that allows one train to pull over, letting a second train get by. A fancy passenger train passed by and came to a stop at the platform where waiting travelers began to gather their belongings in preparation to board the train.

Fearing that the railroad cop might pull the gun which Oliver could see gleaming from his holster, the teenager did as he was commanded. With his head lowered, he sheepishly climbed down from his perch just behind the freight train's engine and crossed the tracks. Several railroad cops were gathering up the handful of hobos who had attempted to hitch a ride, free of charge, on the big freight train. Fifteen-year-old Oliver walked slowly, avoiding any eye contact with the cops, to the back of the line.

"There's a cold jail cell waitin' for you freeloaders," one railroad cop called out in disdain.

Glancing behind him, Oliver saw the line of people waiting to board the passenger train and he quickly came up with a plan. The minute the railroad cops were distracted, he slipped out of his line headed for jail, and silently joined the line of paying customers. Oliver reached up and slowly removed his cap, trying to change his appearance. Keeping his eyes away from the line of hobos and standing very still, Oliver counted his lucky stars when he caught a glimpse from the corner of his eye of the hobos marching off to jail. He breathed a long sigh of relief.

As the passengers began shuffling forward to board the train, Oliver scooted out of line, circled around behind the passenger train and quickly headed back towards the freight train. So as not to be seen, he crouched down in the tall grass on the far side of the track and waited patiently for the passenger train to pull out of the station. As the freight train sounded its long low whistle, announcing its departure from the siding, Oliver waited for just the right moment. Running alongside as the train picked up speed, he reached up to the steel handles just behind the engine, pulling himself aboard.

"Whew! That was a close call," Oliver said to himself. "I can't let that happen again. I might not be so lucky the next time."

When the freight train slowed to a crawl at the next several small towns, Oliver would peer around to see what side of the track the town was built on. Before the train stopped, he would jump off the opposite side and hide in the tall grasses unseen by the railroad cops. When the train was ready to start up again, Oliver would run alongside and jump back on.

This method of travel was working well until Oliver began to get tired and weak. He had started this adventure at midday with nothing more than a pound of gingersnaps in his pocket. It was late afternoon Oliver figured, as he glanced at the sun lowering in the western sky. It wouldn't be too much longer before the sun would disappear off the horizon. Oliver knew he needed a new plan.

As the train pulled into another siding to allow a passenger train through to the station, Oliver had an idea.

"I need to quit this freight train," he whispered to himself.

As the train slowed, he dropped from behind the engine and rolled into the tall grass. Oliver lay there quietly while the travelers boarded the passenger train.

"Think...think!" He said to himself. "What'll I do?"

As the passenger train began pulling slowly out of the station, Oliver did the only thing he knew how to do. Instinctively he ran along the prairie side of the train, reached up for two railings that ran along the sides of the passenger train doors, and hoisted himself aboard. With a place to rest his feet, and a rail to wrap his arm through, Oliver found renewed strength.

"I reckon I can ride this way at least until dark," he reasoned to himself.

As the passenger train whizzed along at forty to fifty miles per hour, the cooling air of evening slapped hard at Oliver's face, keeping him awake. He followed the same routine of jumping off and hiding in the grass each time the passenger train slowed to stop at a town, exchanging travelers. As night fell and only the faintest bit of evening light shown in the Kansas sky, Oliver saw a wide turn in the track ahead. As the train sped along through the turn, he closed his eyes and mouthed a silent prayer.

"Please God, don't let that conductor look out a window now," he begged. "He'll spot me hangin' onto this door for sure."

Just as Oliver opened his eyes, he saw the conductor's head emerge from the window of the first passenger car behind the engine.

"I'm caught, oh geez, I'm in trouble now!" panicked Oliver.

Within a minute the conductor had traveled through the passenger cars reaching the car onto which Oliver clung for dear life. Unlatching the door and sliding it open just enough to reach out, he grabbed Oliver and yanked him onto the train.

"What in the blazes do you think you're doin'!" the conductor scolded him. Kicking Oliver in the seat of the pants, he pushed him towards the back of the train. "You tryin' to get yourself killed or somethin'?"

The conductor pushed and shoved Oliver through several cars until they reached the last car of the passenger train – the smoking car. This was the only car in which passengers were permitted to smoke and it was dark and smelled badly. Putting Oliver in the last seat, the conductor left for the front of the train, mumbling as he went.

Finally able to sit, Oliver realized just how exhausted he had become. As he curled up in the seat with his head resting against the window, he drifted off to sleep. His last conscious thought was that he should probably thank God for not answering his prayer. He needed to be found.

****

"Come on, sonny. You'll have to get off here now," the conductor said as he nudged Oliver from a deep sleep.

As he rubbed his eyes and sat up in his seat, Oliver took a few seconds to remember where he was. The morning sun shone brightly through the passenger train windows. Squinting, he looked around slowly as the events of the previous day came back to him.

"Did I sleep here all night?" Oliver wanted to know.

"That you did. Now get yourself up and off this train. We're changin' engines, and then we'll be

Colby, Kansas Railroad Depot

pullin' out," the conductor told Oliver. "And stay away from these passenger trains. There's a freight train pullin' out right after we leave. Get on that, and be careful. You look awful young to be ridin' these trains by yourself."

Oliver took the conductor's advice and headed towards the freight train. He was groggy and disoriented and his stomach was beginning to ache from emptiness.

"Gosh," he thought to himself. "They let me ride that passenger train till the sun came up. I guess they felt sorry for me."

Walking towards the freight train in the distance, Oliver glanced up at a sign post nailed to the platform. It read COLBY, KANSAS. Just underneath was a second sign that said GOODLAND – 45 miles.

"Goodland, why that's only about thirty miles from Colorado," Oliver said out loud to no one. "I must've rode that passenger train pretty near two hundred miles!"

With that he ran around behind the passenger train and headed for the back of the freight train. Before he could reach it, the freight train slowly began pulling away. Oliver knew he had to be on that train so he started running just as fast as he could. Reaching the open boxcar door, he was startled to see ten or fifteen hobos inside. Two of them reached out and grabbed Oliver by the shoulders yanking him into the car.

"Thank you kindly," Oliver said as he looked over the situation.

"You headed to the harvest fields for work?" one hobo asked.

Oliver thought for just a moment. It sounded like a good idea to him. "Yep," he replied. "That's just where I'm headed."

CHAPTER TWO:
HOW DID I GET HERE?

As the hobos settled into the loose straw which lined the boxcar floor, Oliver took a seat in the doorway where he allowed his legs to swing over the side. A quiet peace settled over him as he looked out at the passing prairie. What a beautiful country, he thought to himself.

All at once the memory of another train ride crept into Oliver's thoughts. In 1906, when he was just shy of eight-years-old, he and his five-year-old brother Edward had taken their first train ride. They had been living in the New York State Orphanage for a year when they were both chosen to ride The Orphan Train from New York City to Kansas. Because of overcrowding in the orphanages, many homeless and orphaned children were being sent west to be placed with farming families. Oliver remembered how he and Edward had made a pact to stay together, no matter what.

"Some promises just shouldn't be made," Oliver said quietly.

After three days on the Orphan Train, Oliver remembered how he and Edward had been chosen by farmer Blaur and his wife. Since the Blaurs had no children of their own, they needed boys to help

MAIN ST. LOOKING WEST
IONIA, KAN.

Ionia, Kansas—Edward's Second Home With William Gish

with all the farm chores. Oliver and Edward seemed like a good choice, but after just one year, the Blaurs abruptly decided that they could no longer keep the Nordmark brothers on their farm. Oliver and Edward were taken back to the train station to ride the Orphan Train a second time. When the train stopped a hundred and fifty miles further west in Mankato, Oliver was chosen first.

"I never should've let them two farmers talk us into bein' split up," Oliver thought. The bitterness he felt towards farmer McCammon and farmer Gish at having lied to the boys was still a fresh taste in Oliver's mouth. "I'll never forgive them that lie."

Since Gish and McCammon lived just a day's ride from one another, they had promised the boys that they could visit with each other at least four times a year. As it turned out, Oliver and Edward only saw each other one time over the next seven years.

"That no good, lyin' weasel," Oliver said out loud. "I guess I don't feel one bit sorry 'bout leavin' his brother's pony in town when I jumped that freight train in Esbon."

Was it really only yesterday, July 4, 1913, that Oliver had suddenly made his decision to run off from the McCammon's? He had gone into town, after finishing all the farm work, to meet up with some friends from school. There was to be a big 4th of July celebration, complete with fireworks, and Oliver had been excited about having some fun with his buddies. After fooling around by the creek, the boys heard the low whistle of an incoming freight train and they ran off to hitch a ride as it slowed down, coming into town. As they held onto the sides of the train, the idea had hit Oliver hard. Just like that, he decided that when that freight train pulled out of Esbon, he was going to be leaving with it. He never thought twice. He had a life to lead and maybe even a chance to find his brother, and he was taking the opportunity.

****

Oliver shifted in the boxcar doorway. As he did, he felt the barrel of his .22 revolver in the pocket of his overalls. He took it out and looked it over. It was his one true possession, bought with his own money from the Montgomery Ward Catalog. McCammon never would have let him have a gun of his own, so Oliver had given his friend's address to ship it to when he placed the order. As the train chugged along, Oliver started taking shots at passing telephone poles. He had hit three in a row when one of the hobos saw what he was doing.

"You crazy fool!" You'd better get rid of that thing. Throw it away, throw it out in the grass," the hobo shouted in alarm at Oliver. "You get caught with that thing its thirty days in jail!"

Oliver had no idea he could go to jail for carrying a gun. He surely was not going to throw it away, but he did slip it back into his pocket. Having been to jail for a week when he was living at the orphanage, all because of a uniform infraction, Oliver had no intention of ever going there again.

"The rules," he said to himself. "You must follow the rules. That's the answer to stayin' out of jail and out of trouble in this world. I've learned me that lesson, that's for sure."

Goodland, Kansas Railroad Depot

CHAPTER THREE:
OLIVER'S DREAM

As the heat of the afternoon sun began making the boxcar unbearable, the freight train's whistle sounded their arrival in Goodland, Kansas, just east of the Colorado line.

"Now listen up," one hobo began. "We're not workin' for a penny less than $4.50 a day and board. We gotta all stick to that. If none of us is gonna work for less, them farmers will have to pay what we're askin'. Is everyone in on that?"

Everyone nodded their agreement as the train came to a stop. The hobos, with Oliver among them, climbed out of the boxcar. They found a grassy spot to rest as they waited for the farmers to come into town. This was the heart of the wheat belt and there was plenty of work to be done harvesting the fields.

Oliver lay down on his back chewing a piece of the tall grass. He watched as several black crows circled above him. The heat of the day, coupled with the mesmerizing circling of the crows overhead, made Oliver feel groggy and he slowly drifted off to sleep.

As Oliver entered a deep sleep, he began to hear the voices of a dream as he found himself back on Frank McCammon's farm.

"Hey, Oliver!" called out his friend Hank. "Look at all the nests over in these trees. I claim this section of the creek."

Running over to where Hank stood, Oliver raised his head, watching as the sky blackened with thousands of migrating crows. Oliver and his friends, Hank and Billy, had been in town when it was announced that a bounty had been placed on crows. The numbers had gotten out of control and they were feeding on the farmer's crops, threatening to destroy the harvest.

"Five cents a head," Oliver shouted over to Billy. "We're gonna get rich off of these birds. I claim this section next to Hank."

All three boys staked out their claims along the creek and then settled in to wait as the crows returned to their nests for the evening.

As night fell, the men from the town made their way to the creek carrying their pump guns. Aiming their guns towards the tree tops, they began shooting. The noise was near deafening. The guns popped and the crows squawked as they fell like rain from their perches. Even though it was too dark to see where they were shooting, it didn't matter. There were so many crows that the shooters really couldn't miss.

Oliver, Hank and Billy scurried around under the trees where the fallen crows lay scattered about. With their hunting knives drawn, they quickly chopped off the heads, stashing them into their leather pouches which were slung over their shoulders. They had to work fast.

As the shooting subsided, the boys could hear the angry shouts of the townsmen.

"Get away from them crows! You boys get out of there, them's our crows!" the voices called in Oliver's direction as the boys ran from the creek.

Once they were at a safe distance the three friends sat down to examine their bounty.

"Not bad," Billy suggested. "Not bad at all, I'd say."

"Yeah," replied Oliver. "But I got another idea. A way we can collect even more."

"A legal way?" Hank wanted to know.

"Of course it's legal," answered Oliver. "You won't find me breakin' the law and goin' to jail. No sir, this is perfectly legal."

"Let's hear it then," Hank said.

"Here's what we do," began Oliver. "We come back in the morning see, when the adult crows are out of the nests huntin' for food. We climb up the trees and get the hatchlings before they can fly. Who knows how much we'll be able to add to our bounty – probably hundreds!"

"Not bad, not bad at all!" Billy smiled as he spoke.

Hank agreed. "We'll meet back here first thing in the morning."

At the crack of dawn the three friends met up again at the creek and put their plan into motion. Oliver had brought along some boxes and a sack of salt.

"What are they for?" asked Hank.

"I don't feel right about just leavin' the bodies here on the ground," started Oliver. "I'm gonna put 'em in these boxes and cover 'em up with salt to keep 'em from rottin', then I'm gonna bury 'em."

"You're too soft, Oliver," replied Billy. "The bodies will just be food for some other animals. Don't go to all that trouble."

"I'm buryin' the bodies just the same," Oliver shrugged. "It's bad enough we gotta kill these crows. The least we can do is bury 'em."

"Suit yourself," Hank said. "Now let's get to work."

The three boys climbed tree after tree gathering their bounty. It didn't take long before their leather sacks were full. As his friends ran off to cash theirs in, Oliver stayed back to salt and bury the bodies of the hatchlings.

After he finished, he too headed off to town excited to see how much money he had made.

****

Oliver woke from his dream to find a farmer kicking at his foot.

"You lookin' for a job, boy?" the farmer asked.

18

"Yes, sir, I am," replied Oliver looking hopefully up at the farmer. "How much do you pay?"

"We're payin' $4.00 a day and board," the farmer answered firmly.

Oliver remembered what he and the hobos had agreed to on the boxcar. "No, I won't go out for that. I want four and a half a day."

"Well, okay," the farmer shrugged. "If you change your mind, I'll be down there in the Implement Shop."

Oliver got to thinking. "Geez," he said to himself, remembering his dream. "I had me close to thirty dollars in the bank back in Esbon from those crow bounties. Why didn't I think of that before I ran off? Now I only got a few cents in my pocket and I ain't eaten all day."

With that, Oliver rose to his feet and headed off towards the Implement Shop. There wasn't much to think about after all. He needed to eat. He knew if he ran out of money he'd have to do somethin' and he wasn't gonna be doin' no stealin' or anything like that. He hoped that the hobos wouldn't think poorly of him, but he had to do what he had to do.

"I gotta look out for myself," Oliver mumbled.

Entering the Implement Shop, Oliver looked around and found the farmer who had offered him work.

He approached the man saying, "I'll go out with ya for $4.00 a day and board."

"$4.00 it is," the farmer answered. "Name's McColl. Burt McColl."

"Oliver Nordmark," Oliver introduced himself extending his right hand.

CHAPTER FOUR:
A REAL WORKIN' MAN

"So what brings you to these parts, Oliver?" Burt McColl asked as he loaded up his wagon with the tools he had purchased from the Implement Shop.

Oliver hadn't had much time to think about that one. What *had* brought him this far west to Goodland, Kansas? The only thing he knew for sure was that he wanted to get away from McCammon's farm in Esbon. He wanted to get started on a life of his own and most of all, he wanted to find his brother Edward. But before he could do any of that, he needed to get some money in his pockets and food in his belly.

"Just lookin' for work," Oliver replied as he pitched in to help McColl finish loading the wagon.

"Well I got plenty of that to keep ya busy," answered McColl as he stopped to wipe the sweat from his brow. "Wheat fields as far as your eye can see and all of it needin' to be harvested by fall."

"Well, I reckon' I'm up to the task," said Oliver as he mentally added up the money he could expect to make in the next two months.

"Have you finished your schooling?" McColl asked as he tried to size up the young man he had just hired.

"Finished eighth grade," Oliver said proudly. "Even earned a gold star for attendance, so I figure I was there for everything they thought I needed to know."

"Hop on in the wagon then," McColl smiled as he motioned to Oliver. "We'd better get started. It'll be a twenty mile ride northwest out to my ranch and I don't much like ridin' after nightfall."

Oliver settled into the back of the wagon as Burt McColl climbed onto the wagon's flat bench seat. Making a clicking sound from the side of his mouth, the farmer shook the reins encouraging the horse forward. As they pulled away from the small town of Goodland, Oliver felt a sense of light hearted freedom.

"I'm on my way," he thought to himself. "Nothin' ventured, nothin' gained. And I plan on gainin'."

****

The ride to Burt McColl's ranch was a long one. They passed several other small farms along the way which had peculiar looking buildings. Oliver wanted to ask about them, but didn't want to seem stupid. Finally his curiosity got the better of him.

22

"What are all them dirt buildings for," Oliver asked Burt McColl.

"Dirt buildings?" McColl questioned as he looked around. "You mean the sod houses?"

"Is that what ya call them?" Oliver asked.

"Most all the buildings out here are made of sod," began McColl. "We call 'em soddies for short; houses, outbuildings, even barns. In fact, I'm the only farmer out in these parts that has a frame barn. Sod's the building material of choice out here on the prairie. There's plenty of it, and free of charge – no need to be haulin' expensive lumber all the way out from town."

"Makes sense to me," replied Oliver.

This was all new to Oliver so he decided to end the conversation before he made an even bigger fool of himself. Sitting quietly he wondered just how these farmers managed to turn dirt from the ground into buildings large enough to live in. What a lot of work that must be. What kind of tools must they need to get that job done?

"Now this here's the start of my land," Burt McColl said as he broke into Oliver's train of thought. "My daddy bought this land for $1.00 an acre – as far as your eye can see."

Oliver stretched his neck in all directions wondering just how many acres McColl must have.

"I've got four brothers and one sister. You got any brothers, Oliver?" Burt McColl wanted to know.

Oliver looked across the wheat fields with a searching, faraway look in his eyes. He did have a brother. Edward was somewhere out there but Oliver didn't know where. He really didn't want to get into all that with Burt McColl. At least not yet.

"Yeah, I got me a brother but he's back in Esbon," Oliver lied. "He's younger than me."

"Well, my youngest brother's about your age," McColl told Oliver. "You'll be mostly workin' with him. His name's Walter but we all call him Walt."

"Sounds good to me," Oliver replied as he gazed out across the wheat field. "That sounds good to me."

****

At his first dinner in the home of Burt McColl, Oliver learned all about the way in which wheat is grown, as well as the type of work he would be doing bringing in the harvest.

"Now there's a number of operations involved in the production of wheat," Burt McColl began in an authoritative voice. "It all begins with preparing and tilling the soil. Next we plant the seed and help the crop grow. Come harvest time, which is where we are now, we start with cutting off the ripe plants. Next we bind the wheat stalks into sheaves and then stack the sheaves into shocks in the field. When all that's done, we'll begin bringing the sheaves into the barn for threshing."

"Threshing?" Oliver questioned.

"That's where we separate out the grain to be sent to the mill for grinding," replied McColl as his younger brother Walt snickered at Oliver's lack of knowledge.

Oliver bit his tongue. He didn't want to lose this job before it even got started.

"We'll be startin' at the crack of dawn," McColl warned. "So I suggest we all get a good night's sleep. It'll be some long days from here on out."

****

Even before the dawn, Oliver awoke to the sound of a rooster crowing. He had been given a place in the loft of the barn to sleep and store his few possessions. He had carefully hidden his .22 revolver deep in the hay and used the blanket that Mrs. McColl had left for him to cover the spot, making a comfortable bed. He had slept soundly and found himself wide awake and eager to start earning his wage as a real workin' man.

"No more free labor from Oliver Nordmark," Oliver said to himself. "Anyone wants a day's work from me, they'll have to pay for it from now on. And I'll give 'em a good day's work no matter what they put me to, but now I'm doin' it for me."

With that Oliver hopped up, washed his face in the water trough and headed for the house. After a filling, hot breakfast with the McColl family, the men headed out to the barn.

"Now this here's the Reaper," began Burt McColl who never tired of talking farming, especially when it came to machinery and the latest type of equipment. "Cuttin' the grain used to require the use of sickles and cradle-scythes, but not anymore. All that stoopin' and bendin' for acre upon acre is a thing of the past. With this Reaper, I just hitch up two of my best horses and lead them along through the fields. See this cuttin' bar?"

Oliver bent down to look at the underside of the Reaper where McColl was directing his gaze.

"Now all those knives on the cuttin' bar are powered by this wheel on the machine. That bar will cut off the wheat stalks real close to the ground."

"What do me and Walt do?" Oliver asked, anxious to get started.

"I'm getting to that," McColl replied. "After the stalks are cut, they fall onto this wooden deck and are swept off onto the ground in a continuous path. You two will rake up the stalks into bundles – we call them sheaves - about as big around as your arms can reach, and tie them up with twine. Once you have six sheaves, you stand them up and lean them against each other with the heads up – that's called a shock. Any questions?"

"Yeah, I got a question," Walt spoke with his head cocked to one side and his hands in his pockets. "Is it quittin' time yet?"

"Very funny," McColl flatly responded. "Let's get to work."

With that, they all left the barn and headed for the fields. Oliver quickly learned the skill of gathering the stalks into sheaves, binding them with twine and stacking them skyward in groups of six. The work proved to be grueling as the morning wore on. The heat of the sun beat down and the tedious task of raking and tying began to cause his arms and hands to ache. But Oliver was used to hard work and he kept up his pace right through until lunch time. Walt, on the other hand, was over fifty yards back from Oliver and falling further behind. Oliver could tell that this youngest of the McColl brothers was a lazy kid, obviously not wanting to do any more than he had to. Burt McColl pulled his horses and the Reaper to a stop. Climbing down off his seat, he walked back towards Oliver motioning Walt to run up and meet him.

"What in the dickens is going on here you lazy cuss," McColl shouted his disapproval at his youngest brother.

"Look at this kid," McColl pointed at Oliver. "Half your size and doing more than a man's work! And you – you're doing hardly nothing compared to him."

Binding and Shocking Wheat in Goodland, Kansas

Grabbing Oliver's hand, Burt McColl continued, "Look at these hands. Rough as leather with the calluses of a man who knows the meaning of a day's work. You could learn a thing or two from someone who knows how to work like that, Walt."

Shaking his head in disgust, Burt McColl unhitched the horses and headed towards the farmhouse for the afternoon meal. Walt too headed for the house, but Oliver just stood there in the middle of the wheat field unable to move. He felt ashamed as he repeated Burt McColl's words over and over in his head. This was a new experience for him. Having his work ethic compared to Walt's for the purpose of making Walt feel bad, even worthless, left Oliver feeling bad himself. Should he slow down and keep pace with Walt? Should he keep working hard and hope that Walt would start working harder too? He didn't want to be fired. He needed this job if he was ever going to have enough money to start looking for Edward. He had hoped to become friends with Walt but slowly he began to realize that he would need to make a choice. Oliver knew that he would always choose Edward so working hard was the answer. Friendship was going to have to wait.

CHAPTER FIVE:
OLIVER'S NEW JOB

Oliver worked for Burt McColl during the harvest of 1913. He quickly became skilled at all aspects of bringing in the wheat crop and earned $156.00 for himself in the process. As August came to a close and the work was finishing up, Oliver knew that he would soon be moving on. Another opportunity, however, was about to present itself.

As he worked one Saturday afternoon at cleaning up the harvesting equipment, Oliver was approached by Burt McColl's brother John with an offer.

"Well Oliver, my brother tells me you were a great help bringing in the wheat crop," John McColl said as he stood with arms crossed over his chest. "Now that the harvest is all but complete, what are your plans?"

"No set plans really," Oliver replied. "I guess I'll be headin' back to Goodland, then maybe ride east a bit."

"What about workin' for me?" John suggested. "I've got some land north of here that I need to put a house on before my wife will head up there with me."

"I don't know nothin' about building houses," Oliver said in a puzzled voice. "I don't know how much help I would be for that."

"Well, I plan to build a sod house, which I've done before, so what I need is a hard worker to help me with the lifting. Now I can't be paying the same as my brother, but I can offer you $30.00 a month and board. What do you say?" John McColl asked hopefully.

Now of course Oliver had stretched the truth a bit when he told John that he had plans to head back to Goodland. He really had no plan at all, and certainly there was nothing in Goodland for him. A few more months of work would bring his savings up well over $200.00 and he would need all of that and maybe more to start his search for Edward. Burt McColl had been a good man to work for and although Oliver had only met John a few times since he had been there, he hoped that the two brothers were cut from the same mold.

"Okay, I'll go out with you," Oliver decided.

"Great!" John replied with a sigh of relief. "We'll head out the first of the month. I'm sure Burt will let you stay here in the loft until then. I'll go and run it by him."

The two shook hands and John headed out of the barn towards his brother's house. Oliver got back to the task of cleaning the Reaper, feeling very lucky that his future was settled – at least for the next few months.

****

The first of September was a dreary, rainy day with a light fog settling on the prairie. John McColl arrived bright and early in his horse drawn wagon loaded with all sorts of supplies. There were building materials and tools, canvas tarps and poles to build a temporary shelter, cooking supplies and more. Oliver noticed a large sled-like object and wondered to himself why they would need a sled. He decided to wait and find out, rather than ask questions just yet.

Bidding farewell to Burt McColl and his family, Oliver loaded his few possessions into the wagon and the two of them headed off across the prairie. It was nearly a six hour ride before the sight of a large windmill came into view.

"Home Sweet Home!" John McColl shouted with a big grin on his face.

Oliver was puzzled. "Are we here?" he wondered out loud.

"Yes, indeed," said John. "So far it's just a windmill that pumps water from the well I dug, but with a little hard work it'll be a real home in no time."

Oliver remembered back to his wagon ride from Goodland to Burt McColl's farm when he had seen a sod house for the first time. He had marveled at the thought of making a house fit to live in from the very earth beneath his foot. He could feel the excitement inside him as he realized that he was about to learn how to do just that.

Pulling the wagon near the windmill, John McColl jumped from the wagon and began unloading things from the back.

"We'll set up our tent here against the side of the wagon and rest up tonight," John spoke as he continued unloading. "Tomorrow we'll get started on building the house."

Oliver, who felt no need to rest up, tried to hide his disappointment at having to wait another day to get started. He helped erect the shelter and joined John McColl for a light supper before turning in for the night.

****

Oliver woke just as the morning sun arose in the eastern sky. He gazed across the prairie and breathed deeply of the fragrant sunflowers that dotted his view for as far as his eye could see. John McColl stirred under the canvas shelter, stretched his arms and woke to greet the day.

"What a beautiful morning," John spoke in a hushed tone.

The rays of morning sunshine danced along the tips of the dew covered prairie grasses creating beautiful prisms of light and color. Both John McColl and Oliver sat quietly for a long moment taking in the beauty before them.

"A perfect day to build a house," Oliver spoke, breaking the silence.

"A perfect day it is," John replied. "What do you say we have some breakfast and head out to find just the right place to start cuttin' sod?"

"I'm ready for that," Oliver smiled.

****

Building a house of sod turned out to be very hard work. The first thing that needed to be done was to find a large level area of prairie where the grass was real thick. Thick grasses would mean a dense, continuous mat of roots that would serve to strengthen the bricks of sod. Using long handled sickles, the grasses were then cut down low to the ground and hauled off. Oliver and John McColl worked in half acre parcels. By the end of the first week, they had cleared off one and a half acres of prairie grass which would produce enough sod to make a small house.

Next came the task of cutting the earth in the shape of bricks. On the morning of the sixth day, John McColl began hitching up his horses to the large sled that Oliver had noticed in the back of the wagon.

"Now you see this sled," John began in explanation as he turned the sled on its side. "These knives stickin' down on each end of the underside are going to cut down deep into the ground. Once we get the whole area cut side to side, then we'll cut the other way, up and down, which will leave the ground cut in the shape of bricks, you see."

Oliver marveled at the ingenuity of this process. "What do we do while the horses are pulling the sled?"

"We get the easy part," McColl smiled. "We sit on the sled to weigh it down so that the knives will dig deep and stay deep. I'll take the reins in the front, you sit towards the back."

The two workers headed out to begin cutting their bricks of earth. This time they decided to work in more manageable, quarter acre parcels. The bricks were cut in twelve inch strips about four inches thick. Changing directions, the sled next cut the strips into manageable lengths about three feet long. Finally, a special plow was used that pulled the sod up and flipped it over while keeping the bricks neatly intact. Oliver and John McColl traveled back to the windmill where they removed the bed from the wagon, replacing it with planks of board. This enabled them to load the heavy bricks of sod more easily onto the flat surface, bringing them back to the windmill where a site was chosen to build the sod house.

"Now the way we lay these sod bricks," John instructed, "is lengthwise making a wall about two feet thick. Every few layers we reverse the process and lay crosswise to bind the walls and make them solid."

Kansas Sod House And Windmill

"Grass side up or down?" Oliver wondered out loud.

"Always grass side down," replied John McColl. "Root side up."

Working day after day laying sod in the same fashion a bricklayer would lay bricks, it took nearly a month to raise the walls of the 14 x 16 ft. sod house. A wooden door frame was set in place on the south side of the house and there were wooden frames where two glass windows would eventually be placed. Since the walls of the house were two feet thick, deep cozy seats were created at each window which would become a favorite spot for Oliver to sit and gaze out across the prairie.

As the construction of the little sod house was nearing completion, Oliver looked skyward and began to wonder.

"How are we gonna put a roof on this house?" he asked John McColl.

"Now that gets a bit tricky," John replied. "First we'll need to frame out the roof with cottonwood poles, and then we'll cover the poles with willow brush and hay. I've got a roll of tar paper which will go over the hay to try and keep the rain out as much as possible. On top of that we'll lay a thinner layer of sod. If we can get some clay, we'll tamp a layer of that on the very top."

"That sounds like it'll take quite a while to finish," Oliver observed. "We'd better keep workin' to get it done before the weather gets bad."

"Oh, we're going to keep working alright," John McColl spoke as he looked skyward. "I need to get this house done so I can start on a barn for the cattle I plan to bring out here."

"I can help you build the barn too," Oliver offered. "That is if you want me to stay."

John McColl smiled. "Now I was hoping you might consider that."

Oliver and John McColl grinned at one another acknowledging that Oliver was doing a good job and that the two of them were enjoying working together. Feeling satisfied with their working arrangements, they put their minds and hands back to the task of completing their house of sod.

CHAPTER SIX:
LIFE IN A SOD HOUSE

Oliver and John McColl finished building their house of sod by the second week of October, 1913. The interior of the small house had two rooms divided by a partition. The front door entered into the kitchen where there was a table with four chairs and a stove for cooking. John McColl brought the stove from his father's house in Goodland. The second room was a bedroom with two beds and hooks jammed into the sod walls to hang clothes on. One bed had a curtain attached that could be pulled closed for privacy. This is where John McColl and his wife would sleep. The second, slightly smaller bed would be for Oliver to share with John's young son Joseph. The floor of the house was dirt which turned to mud whenever it rained since the roof had a tendency to leak. Sometimes after a hard rain would end outside, it would continue to "rain" inside the house for another three or four days. This made it especially hard to keep anything clean. The thick walls of the sod house kept the inside warm in the winter and cool in the summer. During the winter the family cooked with kerosene but in the spring, summer

Winter at John McColl's Homestead

and fall, they would fuel the stove with corncobs or cow chips.

Eva McColl joined her husband in the sod house, along with Joseph, as soon as John and Oliver had it complete and furnished. She had only minor complaints about sod house living and seemed happy with her new home. John was happy to have his family all together again and he and Oliver began work on a small barn.

Oliver took a liking to young Joseph for he reminded Oliver of his brother Edward. He let Joseph tag along when Oliver would take the wagon out onto the prairie to collect the cow chips for fuel. Oliver and Joseph would pick up the cow chips, burnt dry from the sun, like a pancake, until they had a wagon full. Oliver was surprised at how well the cow chips would burn and without a trace of their original scent.

One night, not long after everyone had fallen asleep, Oliver woke to what felt like biting on his toes. As he sat up, he felt something move followed by a loud rumbling sound like a herd of running cattle. He quickly reached for the kerosene lamp.

"UGH!" Oliver screamed. "Rats, rats! There's rats everywhere."

Joseph sat up just as John McColl was bringing another lamp into the room. Rats were all over the bed and running across the floor headed for the holes they had dug into the sod walls.

"Momma, Momma," cried Joseph in a panic.

Eva quickly removed Joseph from the bed and carried him into the kitchen.

"Sorry about that," Oliver apologized as he and John shooed the last of the rats from the room. "They just took me by surprise biting on my toes like that."

"It's okay," replied John. "We'll have to get to work tomorrow filling up all those holes. That'll be a regular task now that colder weather is coming."

Ah geez," said Oliver in disgust as he looked down at his shoes lying by the bed. "They've been chewin' on my shoes."

"Well that's a lesson for you. You'll want to tie the laces together and hang them from the bedpost so they can't do that again," John advised.

John and Oliver joined Eva and Joseph – who was now wide awake – in the kitchen for a cup of tea as they all calmed down from such an exciting start to the night.

****

Oliver stayed with John McColl and his family through the winter and into the spring of 1914. The time passed quickly since there was always so much to do. They finished the sod barn for the small herd of cattle that John had brought to his homestead. In the spring they put in a vegetable garden to help feed the family. By early summer Oliver could feel change in the air.

"Oliver, I need to talk to you," began John McColl as the two headed out of the barn. "I'm afraid I'm not going to be able to keep you on much longer. We've got another baby on the way and things will be getting mighty crowded in this small of a house. Not to mention I'm running out of money to keep paying you."

"I've been thinkin' it's about time for me to be movin' on anyway," Oliver lied. He had become used to living in the sod house and he was genuinely fond of John McColl and his young family. He would be sorry to leave.

"Well then, the timing is right," John continued. "You can stay on for another couple of weeks while you decide what you're going to do."

"Thanks, I appreciate that," replied Oliver as they reached the house. "I'll be movin' on soon."

Oliver on Horseback at John McColl's Ranch

CHAPTER SEVEN:
ONE MORE McCOLL

On the evening before Oliver was to leave John McColl's home, John's oldest brother Doc McColl arrived at the door of the sod house just in time for supper. They all shared a last meal of chicken and potatoes talking lightheartedly about their past year together.

"Yeah, I wasn't so sure what I'd got myself into," Oliver snickered. "I never knew nothin' about building a house of sod, but the money sure sounded good."

"Oh I knew you'd be a big help getting the house built," replied John. "My only worry was whether or not you'd stay on after that episode with the rats!"

"I hate rats," little Joseph piped in. "Oliver has to fill the holes so the rats won't eat me in the night."

"I'm afraid I won't be fillin' no more rat holes, Joseph," Oliver smiled at the boy. "Your papa's gonna have to take over that job. I'm gonna be movin' on in the morning."

Joseph looked sadly towards Oliver as tears welled in the corners of his eyes. His momma had explained to him that Oliver would be leaving soon but that didn't change the fact that Joseph would surely miss his only friend whom he had come to look upon as a big brother.

"It's okay Joseph. You're a big boy now so your papa's gonna need your help around here," Oliver said coaxing a smile from the five year old. "And soon you'll be the big brother of the house."

Oliver wanted to say that the two of them would see each other again but he was hesitant to make a promise that he might not be able to keep. He would always remember the promise he had made to his brother Edward – the promise to stay together was a promise that Oliver just couldn't keep. He knew now that it hadn't been his fault, but he felt responsible nonetheless for the heartbreak that had followed. No, he wouldn't make any promises to Joseph. Oliver was good at learning life's lessons.

"Where ya headed?" Doc McColl asked as he broke into Oliver's thoughts.

"I guess I'll catch a train out of Goodland and head back towards Esbon to look for work," Oliver replied. "Somethin' may come up along the way."

"How about something right in Goodland?" suggested Doc McColl. "My place is about fifteen miles outside of town and I could use a good pair of hands. I can pay you same as John here, thirty dollars a month and board. What do you say?"

"I say you got yourself a hired man," smiled Oliver.

****

Oliver headed off to Goodland with Doc McColl the following morning. As he waved good-bye to John McColl, his wife and young son Joseph, Oliver thought reflectively on his time in the sod house. He had managed to bring his savings from $156.00 to $372.00. He had needed to spend some of his earnings on a winter coat and a new pair of shoes. He had two pair of overalls and two shirts now and he had also purchased socks and underwear. He figured he would work for Doc McColl for awhile and hope to bring his savings up to $500.00. If he had that much he figured he would be able to start his search for Edward.

"What kind of crops you puttin' in Mr. McColl?" asked Oliver breaking the silence.

"First of all, you need to call me Doc," began his new boss. "Everyone calls me Doc, even my own children. I can't think of anyone who calls me Mr. McColl so there's no reason for you to start." He smiled in Oliver's direction then continued. "I'll be puttin' in wheat, barley and oats. After all the crops are in, we'll be starting work on a frame house – one of the first in the area. I've got a sod house now. It's a real nice one but my family's growing and I think it's time to move up to a frame house. So if you're up for it after the crops are in, you can stay on and help with that."

"I'm up for it," Oliver said with a smile. "I'll be lookin' forward to learnin' how to do that."

****

Oliver settled in at Doc McColl's place and worked the planting season. It was hard work but nothing Oliver wasn't used to. Doc's plans to get started on the new frame house that winter had to be put on hold when he came down with severe stomach pains. After a trip to the local doctor in Goodland, he was rushed to Kansas City for an operation to have his appendix removed.

It was up to Oliver to see that all the work got done on the farm while he was gone. Since the crops were in, this meant taking care of the cattle and other animals. One stormy winter day as Oliver tried to pump water for the cattle, the little gasoline engine that powered the pump started missing and backfiring. He had learned a thing or two about gas engines over the course of the last year and a half so he started to tinker with it. He wore a hand-me-down pair of mittens with ragged edges and his fingers were just about numb from the freezing cold. Just as Oliver pushed down on the governor to make it go faster, his stringy mitten caught in the gears. Before he knew what had happened, the gears had taken the end of his thumb off – nail and all.

Numbed from the cold and shocked at seeing the tip of his thumb missing and blood everywhere, Oliver tried to stay calm and take control of the situation. He rushed to the telephone and quickly called Doc McColl's brother Burt who lived about a mile away.

"Burt McColl?" Oliver asked in a panic. "It's me Oliver Nordmark over at your brother Doc's place. I tore my finger off in the pump engine. It's tore clean off and bleedin' everywhere!"

"Calm down Oliver," an anxious Burt replied. "I'm on my way. Wrap it in a clean rag till I get there."

With that the line went dead and Oliver looked around for the cleanest rag he could find, squeezing it on the top of his thumb.

When Burt McColl arrived in his old jalopy Ford, he helped Oliver inside and quickly headed off to the nearest doctor who was about fifteen miles away.

"This storm's a bad one," observed Burt McColl. "You hold on tight and keep the pressure on that thumb."

"I will," shivered Oliver. "But it's pulsing with pain."

Freezing rain and ice poured down on the old jalopy making it harder and harder for Burt McColl to see where they were going. Suddenly and without warning the steering gave way and Burt lost all control. The car veered to the right and took on a mind of its own sliding around on the ice. Finally coming to a stop, Burt tried to steer the old Ford back onto the road but the tires could not get traction, spinning wildly in place. Burt McColl finally let up off the gas.

"We're stuck," he said somberly. "You'll have to get out and help me push to get off this ice."

Oliver glanced down at his aching, torn thumb. He tried his best to tuck his hand up into his coat sleeve, pulled his collar up around his neck and opened his door. The freezing rain was coming down in sheets that seemed to instantly drench him the moment he stepped out of the car. As Oliver ran around to the back, Burt opened his window and yelled to him.

"On the count of three, now. One, Two, Three!"

Oliver pushed with all the weight of his shoulders trying to protect his injured thumb. The old Ford struggled on the ice spewing exhaust in Oliver's face and kicking up ice and water. Finally it lurched forward.

"Get in, we're moving!" yelled Burt from the driver's seat.

Oliver ran to jump in the passenger side as the door flung wildly in the wind. As he reached to slam the door shut, he felt the wooziness of unconsciousness creep over him as he passed out from exhaustion and pain.

****

Spring seemed to arrive overnight in Goodland Kansas that winter of 1915. Doc McColl had recovered from his surgery and Oliver had survived the loss of his thumb tip. Burt McColl had managed to get the unconscious teenager to Dr. Heald's office in Goodland where he was revived with smelling salts. The doctor then proceeded to trim off the wound with a pair of scissors, apply an antiseptic salve and wrap it tightly closed. With time, he told Oliver, the skin would grow together sealing off the wound.

It was mid April when Doc McColl approached Oliver about the frame house.

"I'm going to get started on my new house," Doc informed Oliver. "If you're still interested, I could use the help. If not, you'll have to be leaving."

"Oh I'm still interested," Oliver replied. "Half a thumb's not gonna slow me down."

"Now I was hoping you'd feel that way," Doc smiled. "The first of the lumber's scheduled to be delivered by the end of the week."

"End of the week it is then," Oliver smiled back.

****

Building a frame house was more difficult than Oliver had imagined. He didn't have a lot of experience with a hammer and working with a missing thumb tip made handling the tools a bit more difficult. He often missed the nail he was trying to drive into the wood, hitting his left hand

51

instead. He figured he bent and ruined nearly as many nails as those that he successfully drove through the boards. He was frustrated and discouraged. To make matters worse, Doc McColl's son, eight year old Willie, was a devil of a kid who got pleasure out of tormenting Oliver at every opportunity. Doc often witnessed his son's antics, but never intervened. Oliver was reluctant to speak up or complain about the boy since he didn't want to risk losing his job before he reached his goal of earning $500.00. Finally though, the taunting got the best of him.

As Oliver worked hammering nails in the heat of the afternoon, Willie approached him carrying a gas lamp that had been hanging on the wall in the sod house kitchen.

"Hey Oliver," Willie teased as he swung the lamp in front of his face. "Need some more light to see what you're doin'?"

"No, I don't need no lamp in the middle of the day," Oliver said through clenched teeth.

Swinging the lamp again and again, Willie went on. "Are you sure you don't need more light to see them nails?"

"No," Oliver bit his lip. "I'm seeing just fine."

Hearing the exchange between Willie and Oliver, Doc McColl looked over and snickered. Willie was his only son and he was slow to see any wrong in his actions. He was just a boy having fun as far as Doc was concerned.

Oliver caught Doc's gaze expecting that he would finally intervene on his behalf. When Doc turned back to his work without a word of reproach towards Willie, Oliver lost his composure.

"That's enough for me," Oliver said in disgust as he threw down his hammer. "I'm quittin'."

No one said a word as Oliver headed towards the sod house muttering to himself and shaking his head. He came back out of the house with his bag of possessions in hand and began walking in the direction of town. Doc McColl said nothing as he looked up from his work to see Oliver walking off.

As the afternoon sun lowered in the sky, Oliver continued on his fifteen mile hike towards Goodland. The more he walked, the less frustrated he became and the more he started looking forward. As he lay under the night sky of the Kansas prairie he drifted off to sleep with thoughts of Edward.

"I'm finally on my way," he thought to himself. "I don't have quite as much money as I had hoped to have, but it's enough to get started."

****

Oliver woke at the first hint of daylight. He felt a little tickle on his arm and lifted his head to see what it was. He was surprised to find a little garter snake coiled up right next to him.

"Well, little fellow," he spoke to the snake. "I guess you're all alone and looking for a cozy place to sleep too."

Oliver sat up and continued his one sided conversation with his new acquaintance.

"You know, I'm not afraid of any snake – especially a harmless little garter like you - so you don't have to worry about me tryin' to kill you or nothin'. I come up against a rattlesnake once you know. I was riding an old mare, see, and the mare seen the rattler first and froze up stiff. Slow as could be I got down off that mare, took the rein off and SNAPPED that rattlesnake on the top of his head till he coiled up with his head in the middle. Then I flipped him over, grabbed him and put him in a sack."

Looking down at the garter snake, Oliver went on with his story.

"Yep, I had me a rattlesnake in a sack. I was just new to workin' at Doc McColl's place and after I took the cows in, I took that sack into the front yard where he was standin'. 'See what I got?' I says to him all innocent like. And I threw that rattlesnake out on the ground in front of him. About near gave him a heart attack I think. Then he says to me, 'Geez, boy, if you do that again you'll be going down the road!' He was not happy with me!"

Looking up at the rising sun, Oliver pondered his time with Doc McColl.

"No," he said out loud. "I don't think me and old Doc McColl were meant to be workin' together. We never saw eye to eye on too much of anything."

Oliver stood and gathered his belongings, being careful not to disturb the little snake.

"See ya later little garter snake," he said as he prepared to continue on his journey. "Have a nice life, and watch out for rattlesnakes and farmers with devilish kids."

CHAPTER EIGHT:
THE SEARCH BEGINS

"I'd like a one way ticket to Esbon, Kansas please," said Oliver to the ticket agent behind the train station window.

"That will be $12.68 young man," the agent replied as he took Oliver's money and handed him a boarding pass. "Train leaves in a little more than an hour."

Oliver looked around and spotted a General Store where he bought himself a sandwich and took it back to the platform, settling in for a bite to eat. He glanced down at his ticket with pride as he remembered all he had accomplished in the last two years. He would spend this train ride seated comfortably on the velvet seat of the train car. No more hanging onto the outside of the car trying to stay awake. This time he would arrive at his destination refreshed and well rested. And this time he actually had a destination. Oliver had decided on his walk to Goodland that he would begin his search by going back to visit Frank McCammon in Esbon. His hope was that McCammon would have some answers as to Edward's whereabouts.

"All aboard!" the train conductor called out grabbing Oliver's attention.

He rose from the platform and followed the small crowd of waiting passengers onto the train car. He chose a seat about half way down the aisle and settled in for the ride. Not long after the train had pulled out of the Goodland Station, the conductor made his way through the train cars collecting each passenger's boarding pass. Oliver smiled as he sat up straight and handed over his pass. As the train headed east, miles and miles of passing prairie set Oliver's mind to thinking. What would happen when he showed up at Frank McCammon's farm? He had left so abruptly that 4th of July in 1913...would McCammon even speak to him? What about the pony that Oliver had left in town that day? Oliver tried not to think about that. Instead he found himself wondering about "Little Red".

"Little Red" was the name that Oliver had given to his pet pig. There had been many pigs on McCammon's farm and one day when Oliver was about twelve years old, a baby pig had managed to get out of its pen. Running through the barn, the piglet found its way under the legs of a milking cow. The cow became startled and stamped the ground with its hind feet, crushing the back legs of the little piglet. Oliver and Frank McCammon had come running when they heard the pained squeals of the baby pig.

"Take her out in the field," McCammon said as he handed the crying animal to Oliver. "Kill it and bury it. There's nothing else to be done."

Looking down at the injured pig in his arms, Oliver knew that those instructions would be difficult for him to follow.

"Can I have it?" he asked hopefully.

"Yes, you can have it," replied McCammon as he shook his head and watched young Oliver cradle the piglet. "But it will die anyway."

Oliver remembered the special care he had given "Little Red", as she came to be called. First he had made small splints and tied them with rags to the young pig's hind legs. With the splints, the piglet could walk slowly around, dragging her legs behind her. Oliver had kept "Little Red" in a box while he was working so that she could not go very far and get into more trouble. Feeling that it was too dangerous to keep the injured piglet in the pen with its mother and six siblings, Oliver nursed "Little Red" back to health himself. He fed his new pet milk from a spoon and spent his free time coaxing her around the farmyard to strengthen her hind legs.

Time went on and "Little Red" got better, much to Oliver's delight. She grew out of her box and soon enjoyed tagging along behind her caregiver, much like a pet dog. Wherever Oliver would show up, there would be "Little Red" waiting for him. If the pig got in the way as Oliver went about his chores, he would give her a shove. But "Little

Red" would roll over, get up and come right back to Oliver's side. When no one was looking, Oliver would pick "Little Red" up and throw her in the granary, letting her eat until her heart was content. He continued to give her milk all the time and she grew to be nice and fat.

"Yep, that was one swell pig," Oliver thought to himself as he rested his head against the train's window and closed his eyes to nap. "I wonder what ever became of her?"

****

On the afternoon of the second day, the Conductor announced that the train would soon be arriving at the Esbon Station. Oliver began getting his things together, and then watched out the window to see if he would recognize his surroundings. To his surprise, everything looked about the same as he remembered it.

The whistle sounded as the train pulled into the station. Oliver rose from his seat and followed several other passengers off the train. Standing in the light of day in the middle of town, memories of the six years he had spent in Esbon came flooding back. He remembered having a lot of fun here with his school friends, and he remembered feeling very alone at times without his brother. But mostly, it all felt like so long ago. Even though it had been just two years, in many ways it seemed like a lifetime had passed.

Esbon, Kansas–Oliver's Second Home With Frank McCammon

"Well," Oliver said to himself. "Let's get on with it."

Picking up his bag, he began the seven mile walk towards the farm of Frank McCammon in search of some answers.

****

"Oliver?" Frank McCammon asked with disbelief. "Is that you? Why you're nearly a grown man. Come in, come in!"

Surprised and pleased at McCammon's welcoming smile, Oliver entered the front room of the farmhouse that had once been his home. He took a quick glance around and marveled that everything was just as it had been.

"Are you hungry?" asked McCammon as he headed down the hall towards the kitchen.

Oliver had not eaten since lunch and he knew it was past supper. The walk from town, he now realized, had made him especially hungry. Before he could even answer, Frank was motioning Oliver to sit at the table, while his wife filled a bowl with stew from the stove. They all sat down as Oliver began eating. There was silence at first, and then Frank McCammon spoke.

"That was one bad thing you did," he said. "Leaving that pony there in the stable like that."

Oliver looked up from his bowl feeling instantly like a kid again having his behavior corrected.

""I know it was," Oliver admitted. "But it was tied up and I wanted to catch that train. I just didn't have time to do anything about it."

"Where have you been?" McCammon wondered aloud.

"I've been workin' the last two years straight on ranches around Goodland. I learned how to harvest wheat and how to build a sod house," Oliver spoke with pride. "I even helped build a frame house."

"I hope you earned a fair wage," McCammon said, seaming impressed with all Oliver had learned.

"I saved up near $400.00 before I bought a train ticket back here to Esbon," Oliver spoke as he removed his money from his pants pocket, placing it on the table in front of him.

"Oliver!" Mrs. McCammon gasped. "You shouldn't be traveling around with all that money in your pocket. You have to be awfully careful – especially in the cities – someone will steal that from you."

"I gotta keep it somewhere," Oliver smiled naively. "Can't think of a better place than my pocket."

"Well I can," McCammon replied. "Sewn into your underwear is the best place for a travelin' man to keep his money. Mrs. McCammon here will do the sewin' for you. I'd hate to see you loose that hard earned money to some thief."

"Well, I'd be much obliged," a more sober Oliver replied, realizing that he still had a lot to learn. "I can't be parting with a dime of that money. I figure I'll be needing all that and maybe more to track down my brother Edward."

"Edward?" McCammon raised an eyebrow. "Edward's back east. He hasn't been in these parts for nearly, oh I'd say, six years or more."

"Six years?!" Oliver was shocked. "Why didn't you tell me? Why was he sent back east?"

"Well, now that's a sad story," began Frank McCammon. "But since you're nearly grown now, I guess it's time you heard it."

With that Frank McCammon went on to tell a disbelieving Oliver the events that had transpired beginning in 1907 when Oliver had first come to live with the McCammon's and Edward had gone to live with the elderly William Gish.

The farmers had arranged the first visit for the two brothers about six months after their placements. Oliver had traveled south with McCammon and spent the day at the Gish Farm. When Frank McCammon had attempted to plan a second visit about a year later, William Gish informed him that young Edward had not "met with his expectations" and Gish had been forced to contact the Children's Aid Society to have him removed. When Reverend Swan, the Placing Agent from the Society arrived at the Gish Farm, he realized immediately what had happened. Edward, a boy of just seven, had been forced to do the work of a grown man. When the young boy's back was injured, William Gish decided Edward was no longer of any use to him and would need to leave. Since the farmers who were taking in orphans from the Orphan Trains were looking for farm help, Reverend Swan realized at once that Edward would never be chosen again. He had asked Frank McCammon to house the young boy but money was tight and McCammon was reluctant to take on another mouth to feed. With no other options, Reverend Swan made the decision to send Edward back east where hopefully the New York Orphanage would be able to find him a home.

"So you see," McCammon finished his story. "Edward is back east somewhere, maybe with a new family, or maybe living in the orphanage. There's no telling."

****

Oliver spent the night with Frank McCammon and his wife. As he prepared to leave the following morning, McCammon knocked on the door to his room.

"I'm real sorry about your brother," he began. "I didn't tell you because I knew there wasn't anything that could be done about it."

"Well, there's something I can do about it now," Oliver replied with determination.

McCammon turned to leave the room. "You know," he offered. "You still have that money in the town bank from your bounty hunting. It's not a lot, but it's yours."

"Thanks," Oliver smiled. "I had forgotten about that."

As Frank McCammon left the room, Oliver called out. "Hey, whatever happened to "Little Red"?"

"Oh," McCammon chuckled. "Would you believe she grew up and had young ones of her own? Good thing you were too soft to take her out and kill her!"

Oliver walked away from the McCammon Farm for the last time with enough money in his pocket to get himself to New York City. His savings was sewn safely into his underwear and his belly was full with the warm breakfast that Mrs. McCammon had fixed for him.

"Yeah," he grinned to himself as he walked along. "I did save that little pig's life. I believe old Frank should have offered to pay me for those young pigs!"

As he kicked a small rock along the dusty road, Oliver headed back to town to see about getting a train ticket to the east coast.

CHAPTER NINE:
RIDING THE RAILS

Exiting the town bank in Esbon, Kansas with his $29.77 in bounty money shoved deep into his pocket, Oliver Nordmark decided to splurge a bit as he walked towards the General Store. Once inside, he looked around until he found a display of pocket watches. He was surprised at the range of prices for the various watches and finally settled on the least expensive silver plated one. He made his purchase then headed for the train depot to inquire about a ticket to New York City.

"You can't buy a ticket clear through," the ticket agent informed the seventeen year old. "You'll have to buy a ticket here to get you to Chicago on the Kansas City Rock Island Railway and then buy a second ticket from Chicago to New York City on the Nickle Plate Line. Mind you now, there might be a layover in Chicago before you can catch a train headed out. The whole trip will probably cost you more than forty dollars."

"I've got that much," Oliver replied as he reached into his pocket. "How much for this leg of the journey?"

Train Engine–Circa 1915

"$19.20 to ride from here to Chicago," the agent told Oliver as he looked skeptically at the farm boy before him.

Oliver placed enough money for a ticket to Chicago on the counter and put the rest back in his pocket. Heading for the platform he grew more and more excited about the trip ahead. This would be a three day train ride and he had enough cash in his pocket for the tickets as well as money to eat along the way.

Oliver's trip to Chicago passed uneventfully. He ate and slept on the passenger train and enjoyed the scenery as he gazed out the window. Upon his arrival at the depot in Chicago, he learned that he would not be able to catch a train to New York City until the following morning. Since he had not budgeted for a hotel room, and he didn't wish to open up the stitching on his underwear to draw from his savings, he decided that he would find a spot near the platform and sleep outside for the night. Oliver walked around Chicago's streets marveling at the sights of the big city and stretching his legs before facing another long train ride in the morning. As night fell, he found a spot on the far side of the train tracks, just out of sight from the depot, and settled down to sleep. His travel bag made a nice pillow and Oliver had no trouble falling asleep.

Waking at the first hint of dawn, Oliver sat up and stretched, rubbed his eyes and looked around.

"I suppose I'll look for a quick bite to eat before boarding the train," he thought to himself.

As he entered a local coffee shop, Oliver reached into his pocket for some money. He felt nothing. In disbelief he jabbed his hands deep into all his pockets but the only thing he came up with was a few coins from the pockets of his overalls and his watch which he had tucked away inside his shirt pocket.

"What?" he mumbled to himself. "Where's my…..where's my money?"

Slowly Oliver faced the realization that his money was gone. Thinking that perhaps it had fallen out of his pockets while he had slept, he ran back to the tree where he had spent the night. Pushing the tall prairie grasses side to side he frantically searched the area but found nothing. He ripped through his bag of belongings hoping beyond hope, even though he couldn't remember putting his money in the bag.

After fruitless searching, young Oliver leaned against the tree in despair and slowly slid down the trunk till he was seated on his haunches. He hid his face in his hands as he held back the anger that was raging inside him.

He wasn't sure how much time had passed as he pondered this turn of events, but eventually he lifted his head as he heard a low whistle and looked towards the incoming passenger train. Oliver had planned to purchase his ticket from Chicago to New York City this morning, but now his money was gone and the train would be boarding shortly.

"Some hobo must've stole my money while I was sleeping," Oliver reasoned to himself. "I got no time to unstitch my underwear to use some of my savings. Besides, I'm gonna need that money once I get to New York to live on till I find some kind of work."

As Oliver tried to figure out what to do, darkening storm clouds overhead opened up and a steady rain began to pour. Looking over at the passenger train, Oliver thought and thought until he came up with an idea. He knew that the water tank behind the passenger train's engine had a flat, square grading on top. If he could get up there unnoticed, he could hold onto the sides and ride to New York that way.

"I'll give it a try," Oliver decided.

As the passengers and railroad employees busied themselves at the depot, Oliver ran about a hundred yards ahead of the station through the tall grass. When no one was looking, he stepped out onto the center of the tracks. He began walking towards the train, making no effort to try to hide himself, looking just like any other workin' man headed into town. He had timed the train's departure and as he looked down at his watch, he paced himself just right. The moment that the engine's whistle blew and the train inched forward, Oliver jumped up onto the top of the water tank as he had planned.

"Aw, geez!" Oliver sighed as he reached the top only to find that this tank's grading was round, not square. "This is gonna be harder than I thought. I wasn't expectin' this."

Nevertheless, he laid down on the top of the water tank with his bag slung over his neck and held on tight hoping no one would see him. About a quarter of a block out of the station, he looked up and made eye contact with a couple of fellows standing along the road. They started running towards the train and Oliver knew that he had been caught.

"God help me," he mumbled as he gathered his courage, closed his eyes and jumped from the top of the water tank all the way to the ground below.

Surprised to find himself unhurt, Oliver quickly ran down along the side of the train trying to decide what to do. As a big cloud of steam spewed from the train's engine, Oliver searched for something to grab onto along the side of the train. Finding nothing, he realized that he had no place to go but under the train.

Bending down, Oliver saw a three inch wide beam running the length of the train car. There were two smaller round pipes on either side. Experienced in making quick decisions, Oliver did just that. He crawled up onto the main beam on his belly and grabbed the smaller pipes for balance. It briefly crossed his mind that these one inch pipes might well be steam pipes that would burn him as the train traveled along. Thankfully his luck had changed and the pipes were cool to the touch. Oliver reached back and wedged his bag between his back and the underside of the train car and mentally prepared for the long trip ahead.

Oliver rode wedged on his beam, about three feet above the tracks, from Chicago into Ohio where the train made a stop in Cleveland. He welcomed the chance to relax his grip and wiggle around a bit – something that he didn't dare do while the train was moving at speeds up to sixty miles per hour. Oliver didn't know it, but the brakemen were making their rounds oiling the bearings.

"Hey, get out from under there!" the brakeman yelled in anger when he spotted Oliver in his hiding place.

Not wanting to be hauled off to jail, Oliver squirmed off his beam and out from under the passenger car on the opposite side from the brakeman. He ran as fast as he could and quickly lost himself in a crowd of people. When the train departed the Cleveland station, Oliver ran around to the other side and climbed back onto his perch unseen.

As the passenger train rolled through northern Pennsylvania, its stowaway rider tried hard to fight off the urge to fall asleep. Oliver was growing very tired and twice so far had almost lost his balance. Each time, the thought of nearly dying right there on the tracks was enough to keep him alert for another couple of hours. Finally, when he thought he could hold on no longer, Oliver heard the long awaited sound of the train's whistle announcing its arrival in New York City.

Loosening his grip, Oliver breathed a sigh of relief. "I made it," he whispered as tears of happiness fell silently onto the beam.

CHAPTER TEN:
REUNITED AT LAST

"How much for a ride to Dobbs Ferry?" Oliver asked, peering his head into the window of the red and green paneled taxi car.

"Fifty cents per mile," the driver replied with a smirk. "No doubt more than you can afford."

Gas powered taxis were new to the city and something Oliver had never encountered during his years in Kansas. He had no idea what the fare would cost but figured there was no harm in asking. He quickly decided to stick to one of the horse drawn carriages which were lined up at the train station for a fraction of the cost. But first he would need to have some money.

Walking around the New York City train station, Oliver found a public restroom. Once inside, he huddled into a corner and unhooked the front of his overalls, folding them down to his waist. Silently, he tore at the waist of his underwear until he had worked a small hole into the seam and managed to pull out several bills.

"That should hold me for awhile," Oliver thought to himself.

Quickly he repositioned his overalls, left the restroom and headed for the carriages.

"The Children's Village in Dobbs Ferry," Oliver spoke with authority to the driver. He had learned the location of the orphanage where he had lived as a child from Reverend Swan. Swan was the Placing Agent who had visited him yearly while he lived with the McCammons. He hadn't seen Reverend Swan in over three years but Oliver had committed the information to memory, not knowing when or if he would need it.

Arriving at the front of the Administration Building, Oliver thought he remembered it being much bigger. Of course he had been just eight years old, so everything must have seemed bigger, he reasoned to himself. As he paid the driver and started walking towards the building he heard his name.

"Hello Oliver!" a man called out. "Well look at you, nearly a grown man, welcome back!"

Oliver took a second but then realized that this was Reverend Swan. He extended his hand.

"Grown I am," Oliver replied with a smile as he shook the agent's hand. "Grown and on my own."

"What brings you back to the orphanage?" a curious Reverend Swan inquired.

"Well actually," Oliver began as the two walked along the path leading to the school boys cottages. "You're just the man I'm looking for. I'm trying to find my brother Edward. I was told you might know where he is."

Reverend Swan measured his words carefully, not knowing how much of the story Oliver had

Boys Cottage at The Children's Village of the New York Juvenile Asylum

been told. "Well, he did come back east," the Reverend began. "But he's not here at the orphanage."

"Look," Oliver spoke as he stopped along the path. "I know all about William Gish and how he overworked Edward till he hurt his back and couldn't work anymore. Then he was done with him and you brought him back here. Did you place him with another family or what?"

"He is with a family, Oliver," Reverend Swan offered. "But I don't know where. Once I got him back here, he was out of my care. I suggest you go to the offices of the Children's Aid Society and ask them where he's living."

"Where is that office?" Oliver needed to know. "I'll have to get another taxi."

"No need for that. I'll take you there myself," Reverend Swan offered as he waved Oliver in the direction of his car.

****

Seated across a large desk from the director of The Children's Aid Society with Reverend Swan in the chair next to him, Oliver felt nearly giddy at the prospect of being so close to finding Edward.

"Well now, let's see here," the director began as he searched through the pages of a large roster book. "1908. Yes, here it is. Edward Nordmark returned to The Children's Village due to physical injury."

As the director read from the large book, Oliver squirmed in his chair anxious to hear more.

"Placed January of 1911 with Mr. and Mrs. James Colgrove of Tioga, New York. Here's the street address," the director said as he jotted the address down on a piece of paper and handed it to Oliver.

Looking down at the answer he now held in his hand Oliver felt like he had just won a great prize. Did he dare ask for more?

"What about my sister, Anna? Do you have anything in there about where she is?" Oliver asked courageously. "1905 is when our mother died. Could you check that year?"

The director looked at Oliver over the rim of his eyeglasses. He realized that the young man before him was searching for any connection to whatever family he may have left. He admired Oliver's tenacity.

"Well, now that would be in a different book," the director said as he rose from his seat and walked to a stack of books near the window. "1905... that would be... yes here it is. It should be in this roster book."

Oliver held his breath. It had only just occurred to him to ask about Anna. Would he really be so lucky today as to learn about both his brother and his sister?

"Here it is," the director's voice broke the silence as he read from the book. "Anna Nordmark assigned to the Sisters of Charity

Orphanage in the Bronx section of New York City. There's no notation of a move from that orphanage so I would presume that she is still there. I'll give you that address as well."

Oliver did his best to maintain his composure as he took the second piece of paper from the director of The Children's Aid Society. As he stood to leave, he shook the man's hand vigorously.

"Thank you kindly, sir," Oliver blushed. "Thank you, thank you!"

With that, Oliver and Reverend Swan left the office and returned to the orphanage. Oliver stayed overnight at the suggestion of Reverend Swan to get a fresh start on his next trip the following morning.

With enough money removed from the seam in his underwear to buy a ticket to Tioga, and a bit extra for meals, Oliver boarded the train the next day as he waved good-bye to Reverend Swan.

"Thanks for all your help," Oliver called out from his window.

"Good luck and God's speed, Oliver," the reverend called back. "I hope what you find is what you're looking for!"

As the train pulled off, headed to central New York, Oliver was left to think about what Reverend Swan had meant by his parting remark.

****

Standing momentarily outside the home of James Colgrove, Oliver's memories of his journey to this place raced through his thoughts. A long eight years had passed since he had laid eyes on his brother. Edward was just seven years old the last time the two of them were together. Quickly Oliver added in his head and realized that Edward was now fifteen.

"Well," he said to himself. "Like our father used to say, nothing ventured, nothing gained. Here goes." With that he reached up and knocked on the door.

"Can I help you?" a kindly looking woman asked.

"Yes, I believe you can, ma'am," began a nervous Oliver. "My name is Oliver Nordmark and I have been told that my brother Edward lives here."

"Why yes," a surprised Mrs. Colgrove replied. "Come in, come in."

Oliver entered the front door of the small frame house and took a quick glance around. This was a modest home with neat rooms and simple furnishings. Mrs. Colgrove motioned Oliver to the sofa in the front room.

"You just have a seat here, Oliver," she spoke as she looked Oliver over. "I'll go and fetch Edward."

Several minutes passed as Oliver sat excitedly on the sofa. Finally he heard footsteps in the hall and then he saw him. Edward stood tall and thin with his blonde hair clipped close to his head – but not so close that Oliver couldn't see the hint of the curly haired little boy of his childhood. The brothers stood and gazed upon each other for a long moment. Moving towards Edward, Oliver broke the silence.

"Edward," he began hesitantly as he stepped forward. "It's me, Oliver."

The brothers reached for one another and as they embraced, the years seemed to just melt away.

"Sit down, sit down," Edward smiled as he looked Oliver over. "I can't believe you're really here!"

Mrs. Colgrove quietly left the room to give the brothers some private time to become reacquainted.

"I was sorry to learn from McCammon that old Farmer Gish turned out to be no good. I didn't know they had sent you back east until just last week," Oliver began to explain to Edward. "Soon as I was told, I headed out of Kansas to find you."

"Where you been all this time?" Edward wanted to know.

"Well," Oliver took a deep breath. "I was at McCammon's till I turned fifteen – same as you are now. That's when I couldn't take it no more. I was doin' all the work on that farm and gettin' paid nothing. I figured I could do as much for myself, if you know what I mean. So I hopped a freight train out of town and ended up in Goodland, almost to the Colorado line. I worked for a couple of brothers for two years, saving up my money. Then I went back to McCammon's to try and find out where you were. That's when McCammon told me about Gish."

"What kind of work did you do?" Edward wanted to know.

"Well, I learned how to harvest wheat, and would you believe I learned how to build a house out of the earth? It's called a sod house," Oliver said with pride. "And before I left, I was workin' on building a frame house."

Edward and Oliver sat quietly as each of them considered all they had been through and how their lives had taken such different turns. Finally Edward broke the silence.

"Did you come to take me away from here?" Edward asked with hopeful eyes.

Oliver was surprised by Edward's question and took a moment to reply.

"Don't you like it here?" he wondered aloud. "Looks like a decent place, and Mrs. Colgrove seems nice enough."

"Oh, she puts on a good show. Her and Mr. Colgrove act like they're the pillars of society, if you know what I mean," Edward spoke softly so as not to be heard. "But soon as no one's lookin' they're mean as all get out. I don't know how much longer I can stand livin' here, I can tell you that."

Edward rose and walked slowly to the doorway, checking that Mrs. Colgrove was out of earshot.

Oliver noticed right away that Edward walked with a slight limp; the result of his injuries at the Gish farm, Oliver reasoned.

"What do they do that's so mean?" Oliver questioned.

"Oh, all kinds of things. I could take a week telling you stories," Edward shook his head just thinking about it. "One time when I was out back working on my old bicycle I got my fingers stuck in the chain. It hurt so bad, I was yellin' and screamin' for help but nobody came. I knew they were both in the house, too. I passed out a couple times, the pain was so bad, before old Mr. Colgrove finally got up to come out and see what the trouble was. He went and got a tool to cut the chain, but not before he yelled at me for being so stupid. I nearly lost these two fingers. You can see the deep scars right there."

Oliver leaned over and looked at Edward's misshaped and scarred fingers. His heart felt heavy for his brother who had suffered so badly at the hands of people who were supposed to take care of him. But what could Oliver do?

"I don't know what I can do," Oliver said sadly. "I don't have a job or a place to live myself. And besides, you're just fifteen. If I tried to take you from these people the law would probably be after us both."

"Well," a resigned Edward shrugged his shoulders. "Then the law's gonna have to be after just one of us because I'm not stayin' here."

"Don't do that," a worried Oliver pleaded. "Just a few more years and you can leave without any trouble. I don't want you to end up in jail Edward. Please say you'll hang in here just a bit longer."

"I'll try," Edward said. "But I ain't makin' any promises."

****

At Mrs. Colgrove's insistence, Oliver stayed two nights at the little home on Maple Street, sleeping on the floor of Edward's bedroom. The brothers spent more time catching up on their missing years and talked a lot about their future plans. On the morning of the third day, Oliver packed his small bag to go. Edward watched in silence.

"I'm going to come back Edward," Oliver promised. "I need to find work and a place of my own. Then when you're old enough, you can come live with me."

"I want to believe that," Edward said sadly.

"Here," Oliver said as he reached into his pants pocket and brought out his watch. "Here's my watch. And take good care of it till I come back. And I will be back for it."

Edward took the pocket watch and curled his fingers tightly around it. He looked up at his big brother with moist eyes.

"I'll see you soon," Oliver extended his hand to Edward.

The brothers shook hands, and then embraced a final time.

"I love you Edward," Oliver whispered as he turned and walked from the house.

CHAPTER ELEVEN:
EDWARD'S MISTAKE

Oliver's next destination after leaving Tioga was back to New York City. He went to The Sisters Of Charity Orphanage on Kingsbridge Road in the Bronx section. There he did indeed find his sister Anna who had lived with the Catholic Sisters since 1905. They sat and talked for several hours in the living room of the orphanage getting reacquainted. To Oliver it seemed that Anna was getting along just fine and she seemed to be happy enough.

After several failed attempts to find work in the city, Oliver was approached by a Navy recruiting officer in his temporary home at the Salvation Army Shelter. The recruiter offered Oliver four years of food and shelter, along with a paycheck, for his service aboard the USS Melville, a destroyer in the Atlantic Fleet.

"Are you eighteen?" the recruiter asked. "If not you'll need to have your guardian sign up for you."

"Well I'm not eighteen yet and I've got no guardian," Oliver explained. "I'm on my own you see, so I don't suppose I can sign up."

The recruiter looked around the room and nodded in the direction of the clerk seated at the front desk.

How about that fellow at the desk over there?" the recruiter suggested. "He's old enough to sign for you. No one will know he's not your real guardian."

Always after an adventure, Oliver took just a few seconds to think it through then signed on the dotted line. The clerk was more than happy to sign for Oliver's enlistment. With Oliver in the Navy's care, there would be one more available bed at the shelter.

****

After Oliver's departure, Edward spent about two weeks sulking around the Colgrove's house becoming more and more restless about his situation.

"Oliver was fifteen, same age as me when he hopped that freight train out of Esbon," he reasoned to himself. "I don't see why I have to wait any longer to get away from these people."

The main problem with leaving, as far as Edward could see, was that he didn't have any money and he had no experience with hopping onto trains. Besides, with his back injury, he didn't think he would even be capable of jumping onto a train. He spent days thinking of how he could get a hold of some money to make his break. That Saturday, he saw his chance.

"Edward," James Colgrove called up the stairs. "We're going to visit my brother and his wife for the day. We'll be back around nightfall. I want you to get the grass cut while we're gone and while you're at it, pull some of those weeds growin' by the back fence."

"Yeah, alright," Edward called back from his room.

After the Colgroves were gone, Edward crept around the house looking into every closet, cabinet, box and niche for anything of value. The Colgroves were not a wealthy family by any means, but they were not destitute either. Finally, under James Colgrove's bed, Edward found just what he was looking for.

"Now that's a nice shotgun," he whispered aloud to only himself as he slid the weapon out and placed it on top of the bed. "That ought to be worth somethin'."

Edward carried the gun to his room. He packed a small duffle bag with a few things that he figured he would need to get by. As he looked around his room, his eyes caught the shiny silver of Oliver's pocket watch. Edward snatched it up and slid it into his pants pocket.

"Sorry Oliver," he said out loud. "I can't wait any longer."

With his duffle bag slung over his shoulder and the shotgun tucked under his arm, Edward left the small house on Maple Avenue and never looked back.

****

"No, I don't give cash for guns," the pawn shop owner informed fifteen year old Edward. "But you can make a trade for another gun. That's the best I can offer you."

Looking nervously around the shop, Edward tried hard to decide what to do. As he glanced past the owner's head to the back wall, he saw a row of revolvers displayed. He quickly decided that a revolver would be easier to walk around with than a shotgun.

"Alright then," Edward said as authoritatively as he could. "I'll trade it for a revolver. One of them back there'll do just fine."

The pawn shop owner took a revolver down from the wall and showed it to Edward. He demonstrated how to load the gun, which bullets to buy, and how to clean the chamber. Edward was too nervous to remember a thing the man said.

"Is it an even trade then?" asked Edward wanting to get out of there.

"I'll just need your name on this form and then yes, it's an even trade," the owner said as he placed a pencil and paper in front of Edward. "I'll even throw in a few bullets."

Thinking fast, Edward penciled a name on the line provided and pushed the paper back towards the shop owner.

"Lloyd Mickle," the owner read from the paper. "Well, nice doin' business with you Lloyd. That's a fair trade. Now try and stay out of trouble with it."

Edward nodded in the man's direction, picked up the revolver and quickly exited the pawn shop.

****

With the revolver tucked inside his pants and covered up by his jacket, Edward nervously walked around trying to figure out what to do. His original plan to sell the shotgun to get enough money to buy a train ticket to New York City had not worked out. He still had no money, but he did have the revolver. As he walked away from the center of town, he saw an older, well dressed man sitting on a wooden bench. The man appeared to be alone, so without thinking of the consequences, Edward put an ill conceived plan into motion. Casually, he walked up to the man and spoke.

"Hey, mister," Edward began. "I'm a bit down on my luck. You got any money you could spare me?"

"Get out of here you hobo," the man said with disgust. "Get a job."

"This is my job," a shaking Edward said through gritted teeth as he jammed the barrel of his revolver into the man's side. "Now give me your money."

The man's attitude towards Edward was quickly replaced by alarm and fear. He reached into his pockets and handed over his money as sweat poured from his brow. Edward grabbed the money and took off running.

"Help! Help! I just been robbed!" the man called out as he frantically waved his arms in all directions.

Three men who had been standing a short distance away heard the older man's shouting and took off after Edward. Running as fast as he could, Edward looked several times over his shoulder and realized that the men were closing in on him. As they caught up, the three pursuers pounced on Edward, tackling him to the ground. They wrestled his hands behind his back and hauled him back to town, delivering him directly to the sheriff's station.

The following morning, after a brief trial, Edward stood before the judge who spoke harshly to the young offender.

"Edward Nordmark, you have committed a serious crime," the judge began as he looked directly at Edward over the top of his eyeglasses. "However, due to your young age, and lack of any prior criminal record, I consider you a candidate for rehabilitation. Therefore, I sentence you to a five year indeterminate sentence at the Elmira Reformatory. Do you have any questions?"

ELMIRA, N. Y. ELMIRA STATE REFORMATORY.

Elmira Reformatory–Elmira, NY

"Indeterminate, sir?" a nervous and shuffling Edward asked.

"Yes, young man, indeterminate," the judge responded. "That means that your behavior and speed of rehabilitation will determine the length of your sentence. You will be required to attend classes to complete your education as well as perform labor in one of the Reformatory's Work Shops. When your sentence has been completed, you will be followed by a parole officer of the state for a period of no less than two years."

The judge brought his large gavel down with a bang and stood to leave the room. Edward was then led out by a jailhouse guard to begin his rehabilitation.

CHAPTER TWELVE:
ESTELLA MAY

While stationed on the USS Melville, Oliver decided to write to Edward to see how he was getting along. He was surprised when the letter was returned, two months later, with a hand written message on the envelope.

"No longer at this address. Sentenced to The Elmira Reformatory for five years after committing armed robbery."

Oliver was saddened by the news. What had gone so wrong that Edward would resort to armed robbery? Did he run away and find himself without money for food or shelter? Oliver couldn't make sense of it no matter how hard he tried. Whenever Oliver had been without money to eat, he would go to the back door of a restaurant and ask for some stale buns or bread – or a job for heaven's sake. Never would he have reached for his gun to rob an innocent person. Where did Edward get himself a gun, anyway? The situation weighed heavily on Oliver's mind but there was nothing he could do about it while he was at sea.

When he was issued his first leave papers, Oliver knew just what he would do. He went to the train station and purchased a ticket to Elmira,

New York. As he boarded the train and made his way down the aisle looking for a seat, he caught a glimpse of a young girl smiling up at him. He passed the girl, who was seated next to a woman that he figured must be her mother, and sat two seats back on the opposite side of the aisle. The train pulled slowly out of the station and Oliver settled in for the long ride. Before long, the young girl stood up and walked towards Oliver.

"Can I sit with you?" she asked as she stopped at Oliver's seat.

"I don't care," Oliver responded as he wondered what was wrong with the seat she had been in. "Suit yourself."

"My name's Estella," the young girl offered. "Estella May Rarick."

Oliver glanced over at this skinny little girl not wanting anything to do with her. He wasn't used to being around girls but he knew he shouldn't be rude.

"Oliver Nordmark," he finally answered and then looked out the window.

"Would you like to see my magazine?" Estella asked in her sweetest voice as she offered her magazine to Oliver in an effort to engage him in conversation.

Oliver took the magazine, thumbed through its pages but didn't have anything to say about it. He handed it back to Estella.

"My mother and I are going home to Elmira," Estella tried again. "We've been to visit my aunt in

Stroudsburg, Pennsylvania. Where are you getting off?"

"Oh, I'm going to Elmira too," Oliver said as he looked back towards the young girl. "I got family there."

"That sure is a nice uniform you're wearing," Estella complimented the young sailor. "Are you in the Navy?"

"Yes I am," Oliver said proudly. "I've got two more years at sea."

Estella and Oliver proceeded to get acquainted during the train ride to Elmira. Oliver learned that Estella had worked in a logging camp in Washington State and he shared with her stories of his earlier days in Kansas. When the conductor announced that the train would be pulling into the station in fifteen minutes, Estella got up her nerve to ask Oliver what she really wanted to know.

"If I give you my address, will you write to me when you're out to sea?" she asked hopefully, holding her breath.

"Go ahead," Oliver smiled. "Write it down and I'll send you a letter."

Estella went back to her mother's seat and returned with a pencil. She tore a page from her magazine and jotted her address down, then handed it to Oliver. He folded the paper and slipped it into his pocket.

As the train pulled to a stop in the Elmira Station, Estella stood up and gathered her things to leave.

Estella May Rarick in Washington State–age 14

"Good-bye Oliver," she grinned. "I'll be looking for your letter."

"Good-bye Estella," Oliver replied with a half grin of his own.

****

Oliver sat in the Visitor Waiting Room of the Elmira Reformatory wondering just how this visit with Edward was going to go. He rose from his seat as the door opened and his little brother was escorted into the room. The door shut behind him as Edward lowered his head.

"Edward, what happened?" Oliver broke the silence as he motioned Edward to sit. "I thought we agreed that you would stay with the Colgroves until you were older and I had a place where you could live?"

"I couldn't wait," Edward spoke softly. "I ran off with Mr. Colgrove's shotgun and traded it in at the pawn shop for a revolver. Then, I don't know what came over me, but I tried to beg money from some old guy. When he refused and called me a hobo, I just took the gun and demanded money from him. I don't know why I did it, I was desperate."

Oliver decided to change the subject. There was no use in trying to go back and change anything that had already happened. They'd have to make the best of the situation now.

"So how ya gettin' along?" Oliver asked, trying to sound upbeat. "What's this place like?"

"It's okay," shrugged Edward. "Beats living with the Colgroves to tell the truth. I go to classes and I go to work. I eat and sleep, you know, the regular stuff. And I do a lot of reading. "

"What kind of work do you do?" Oliver asked.

"Well, they got what they call the Piece/Price System of work here. I put together belts and suspenders, hammerin' the buckles on and drillin' holes in the leather," Edward started to become a bit more animated as he spoke about his work. "I make three cents for every completed belt. It's a bit of money, which I never had, and it fills part of the day. It ain't bad."

Oliver and Edward spent about half an hour catching up on one another's lives until the door opened and the guard informed the brothers that their visit was over.

"I'll be out of the Navy in just two years, Edward," Oliver said in parting. "I'll be back as soon as I'm discharged."

"I'll be lookin' for you," Edward smiled as he turned to go. "Don't worry about me, Oliver. I'll be fine here."

****

Back on the USS Melville, Oliver wrote a simple letter to the young girl he had met on the train.

99

"Why not," he figured to himself. "Nothin' ventured, nothin' gained. I got nothin' to lose, and she seemed like a nice enough kid."

He was surprised at how quickly Estella wrote back to him. Her letter arrived with a surprise invitation to spend Thanksgiving with her and her family. Oliver knew that he would be back at the Philadelphia Port in time for the holiday, so with no other plans, he wrote back accepting the invitation.

The train ride to Elmira was packed with holiday travelers. Oliver arrived at midday and quickly found a taxi to take him to the address Estella had given him. He paid the driver and approached the front door with a bit of apprehension. Was this really a good idea he wondered? He barely knew this young girl.

"Well, I'm here now," Oliver shrugged as he reached up and knocked on the door.

****

Oliver need not have worried. Estella introduced him to her mother Emma Rarick and explained that her father had passed away when Estella was just five. She had seven brothers and sisters, he learned, and three of them were home for Thanksgiving. Mary Ann was the oldest of the three with George Jr. next and Henry just in line above Estella who was the baby of the family.

Everyone was very welcoming and Oliver thoroughly enjoyed his visit. He was finally getting a taste of what being part of a real family was like. He now realized just what he and Edward had missed all those years.

"How are you enjoying work in the Navy?" George Jr. asked Oliver at one point during the meal.

"Its exciting work," Oliver answered. "And I'm earning a bit of money which I'm saving for when I get out."

"That's very wise of you," Estella's brother cautioned. "You never can be too careful where money's concerned."

Oliver knew that all too well. He could get by on very little but if he wanted to get ahead in the world he needed to save what he could.

Estella showed Oliver around town after the evening meal and the two young people continued to get better acquainted. When they parted company, Oliver had decided that he liked Estella very much and would continue to write to her while he was at sea. He didn't know where the friendship might lead, but he decided to give it a shot.

****

After a two year correspondence, Oliver felt that he and Estella had gotten very close. Two months before his discharge from the Navy in 1919, he wrote his final letter from the ship.

Dear Estella,

    I know this may be a bit sudden, and you might think I'm being too fast, but I was hoping that when I get back on shore, maybe you would consider getting hitched. I know you'd have to ask your mother since you're not yet sixteen, but if she would be willing to sign for you, we could get married right away. I've got some money saved up that we could live off of till I find a job. I'll wait for your answer when I get into port on April 2nd. I will be coming into Philadelphia and hope that you will be able to meet me. If I don't see you there, I will catch the train to Elmira.

Yours,
Oliver

****

    An anxious and nervous Oliver Nordmark searched the pier as the USS Melville pulled into port. He scanned the crowd, hoping beyond hope that young Estella had gotten permission from her mother to meet him. Most of all he was hoping that Estella would accept his proposal, which would make him the happiest sailor aboard the ship. At last he caught a glimpse of fifteen year old Estella, her mother at her side. She was waving her handkerchief in his direction and her face was flushed and smiling. Oliver took that as a good sign. When the sailors were finally permitted to disembark from the ship, Oliver kept his eyes on Estella so as not to lose sight of her in the crowd.

"Oliver!" Estella called out. Oliver, over here!"

Oliver rushed to greet Estella and the two embraced briefly. Before Oliver could even speak, Estella answered his most pressing question.

"Yes, yes, I'm answering your letter!" she began in excitement. "Mother will sign the papers and we can get married right away!"

Oliver's face filled with happiness; more happiness he was sure than he had felt in all his twenty years.

"Thank you, thank you," he grinned as he shook Emma Rarick's hand a bit too hard. "You won't be sorry. I'll take good care of her. I've got some money saved up and I'm a hard worker so I know I can get a job pretty quick."

"I'm sure everything will be just fine," Emma Rarick smiled back at the happy young man before her. "We'll make the plans as soon as we get back to Elmira."

The three travelers made their way through the crowd to the train station and waited for the boarding call to Elmira, ready to begin a new life.

"Well," Oliver smiled to himself proudly. "Nothing ventured, nothing gained is certainly working out well for me!"

****

Twenty-year-old Oliver Nordmark and Estella May Rarick who was just two months shy of her sixteenth birthday, were married in a small frame chapel in Painted Post, New York on May 10, 1919.

The bride wore a simple white dress with a small floral print and belted waist. The groom wore a clean white shirt adorned with a thin black tie. The service was performed by the local minister, Reverend John Knox. Estella's mother, along with Reverend Knox's wife Eunice, stood as witnesses for the young couple. They received two wedding gifts; a comb and brush set from Estella's best friend Helen Gamble, and a cup and saucer set from Estella's mother.

As Oliver and Estella stepped out of the chapel for the first time as man and wife, Oliver breathed deeply of the sweet spring air. He didn't know for sure what the future would hold, but he knew where he had been and the many life lessons he had learned. Smiling down at his new bride, he looked forward to his chance for a happily ever after.

Cottage "family" out for a ride—Children's Village Orphanage

Oliver Nordmark: 1913 Esbon, Kansas

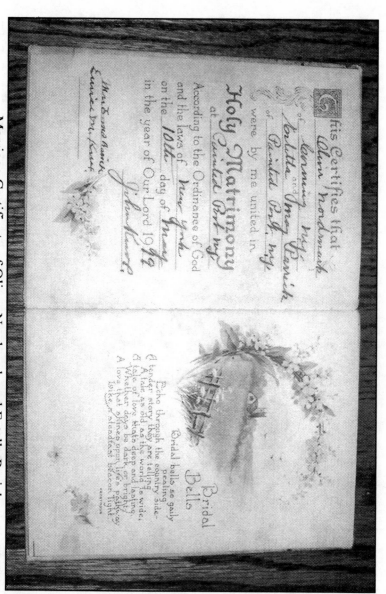

Marriage Certificate of Oliver Nordmark and Estella Rarick

Portrait of Estella Rarick Nordmark, circa 1925, age 21

Oliver and Estella's Children–Back: May & Margaret Front: Francis (Bud), Oliver, James & Benjamin

Oliver's Sister Anna With Her Daughter & Two Grandchildren

Oliver And His Children—Back: Oliver Jr., Benjamin, James & Francis (Bud)
Front: May, Oliver & Margaret

Oliver, Estella and Edward's Final Resting Place in Prospect Cemetery, East Stroudsburg, PA.

EPILOG

Oliver and Estella Nordmark

Oliver and Estella Nordmark settled first in Corning, New York where Oliver found work at a glassworks factory. After being laid off from that job and being unsuccessful in finding another, Oliver reenlisted in the Navy where he received both a "shipping over pay" and a salary. He sent everything he received back to Estella and their first child, May. Estella wrote Oliver several letters telling him she was having a hard time making ends meet. When he returned home for a 48 hr. leave, Oliver decided to leave the Navy and head back to Kansas where he felt certain he could find work. As soon as he got a job following the harvest, he sent for Estella and May. Their second child Francis, or Bud as he came to be called, was born in Kansas. When work dried up, Oliver put Estella and the children on a train back to Pennsylvania. He didn't have enough money for a train ticket himself, so he resorted to riding the rail as he had done when he was seventeen.

The family settled in Stroudsburg, Pennsylvania where Oliver found work and four more children were born – Oliver, Margaret, James and Benjamin. As the Great Depression took hold of the country, work again was scarce. Oliver finally gave in to Estella's pleadings to allow her to pick up work at a local hotel, The Indian Queen, working in the coffee shop. Tragically on the first day of her new job, Estella accidentally fell down a flight of stairs and died instantly.

Try as he might, Oliver was unable to provide for his large family. He relinquished his children to the Children's Aid Society where they were placed in foster care. He continued to stay in contact with them throughout their lives.

Edward Nordmark

In 1939, Edward Nordmark was again arrested for armed robbery. He was sentenced to life in prison at Joliet State Penitentiary in Illinois. He was later transferred to Attica Prison in New York. In June, 1958, Attica Prison made the decision to release Edward due to poor health. He went first to visit his sister Anna in New York then went to live with Oliver in Stroudsburg. On July 1, 1958 at the age of 58, Edward passed away from heart disease.

Anna Nordmark

Anna Nordmark stayed in the Catholic Home in New York until adulthood. She later married and had two children.

<u>Oliver Nordmark</u>

Oliver never remarried and continued to live in Stroudsburg, Pennsylvania. He worked as a silk weaver and as a house builder, eventually going to school to learn the welding trade. He traveled to Pearl Harbor in Hawaii where he worked as a welder on a reconstruction project after the infamous attack in 1941. His adventurous spirit took him all over the U.S. sometimes traveling with family; often traveling on his own. He was outgoing and talkative, making friends wherever he went. Most of his twenty grandchildren knew him well and enjoyed spending time with him. In his sixties Oliver learned to fly an airplane, water skied on the Delaware River, learned to scuba dive in Florida and traveled to Mexico and Ireland where he kissed the Blarney Stone.

In his seventies, Oliver discovered through genealogical research that his mother had not died when he was six as he had been told. In fact, she had deserted her family and died when Oliver was thirteen of Typhoid Fever and alcohol poisoning. It is believed that his father Otto placed the three children with the Children's Aid Society. Otto died of heart disease in 1907.

Oliver Nordmark passed away at the age of ninety-five after being hit by a car while riding his bicycle. He is buried in Prospect Cemetery in East Stroudsburg, Pennsylvania beside his wife Estella and brother Edward. He is survived by four of his six children; Oliver, James and Margaret of

Stroudsburg, and Benjamin of West Grove, Pennsylvania. I am honored to have known him.

---Donna Nordmark Aviles

GLOSSARY

Cottonwood Poles – A type of poplar tree with cottony seeds and strong pole like trunk.

Cow Chips – Pancake shaped, dried cow manure baked hard by the sun and used for fuel.

Cradle Scythes – Tool used for cutting wheat or tall grass. The blade is approximately 27" long and curved slightly upward to optimize the cut. A long handle allowed the farmer to cut without constant bending. Scythes fitted with a cradle or bow not only cut the grain, but would also scoop it up and lay it to the side in a neat path, ready for binding into sheaves. One man could cut three to four acres a day with a cradle scythe.

Governor – Part of the mechanism on an engine that regulates the supply of fuel.

Granary – A building for storing threshed grain.

Leave Papers – Signed papers given to servicemen allowing them to be away from their assigned duties for a specified period of time.

Sickle – Curved blade tool used for cutting wheat and grass in the 1800's. Working with a sickle required a lot of bending, back-breaking work. It would take a man a full day to cut nearly one acre with a sickle.

Smelling Salts – A mixture of ammonia and perfume used to restore someone to consciousness by placing it under the person's nose.

Soddie – Nickname or common name used for a sodhouse in the late 1800's – early 1900's.

Sod House – Small houses built from blocks of sod cut from the earth.

Willowbrush – Trees that grow along creeks and streams that have narrow leaves and strong, lightweight wood.

PHOTOGRAPHIC CREDITS

Joseph Petr Sod House – 1913
Fred Hultstraud History in Pictures Collection
Institute for Regional Studies and University Archives
North Dakota State University Libraries, Fargo

Main Street of Esbon, Kansas
Photographer: Ashby
Collection Name: Images of Kansas Towns and Cities
Wichita State University Libraries, Dept. of Special Collections

Train Depot at Colby, Kansas
Main Street of Ionia, Kansas
Train Depot at Goodland, Kansas
Photographer: unknown
Collection Name: Images of Kansas Towns and Cities
Wichita State University Libraries, Dept. of Special Collections

The Old Sod House
Photographer: unknown
Sod House Photograph Collection

Wichita State University Libraries, Dept. of
Special Collections

Children's Village Cottage
Cottage "Family" Out For a Ride
Westchester County Historical Society Collection

Winter in Kansas
Oliver Circa 1913
Portrait of Estella
Oliver's Children in the Care of The Children's
Aid Society
Oliver and His Grown Children Circa 1954

From the collection of Benjamin E. Nordmark

Binding and Shocking Wheat
Oliver on Horseback
Anna Nordmark, Her Daughter and Grandchildren

From the collection of James B. Nordmark

Estella in Washington State Caring for a Blind
Cow

From the collection of Ed Hall, son of May
Nordmark Hall